The why and how of this book

Every month the Doctor Ann website (**www.teenagehealthfreak.org** and **www.doctorann.org**) receives over 1000 emails from young people from all over the UK asking questions about things that worry them about their body, their life, their health, their parents, and their friends. As well as lots of questions about sex, drugs, bullying and many other subjects, young people write about their relationships. They talk about relationships with friends, both of the same sex and of the opposite sex, with family, with relations and with others in the world around them. This book contains many of these emails and our answers to them. There are questions and answers about how to start relationships, how to move relationships on from being friends to something more where sex may be involved, how to handle relationships when things go wrong, old issues like relationships with adults, especially teachers, and new issues like internet relationships. We have picked out the most common problems associated with relationships, where they go right as well as wrong, and how to handle things along the way so that things work out the best possible way.

The website was originally set up because of the success of the books *Diary of a Teenage Health Freak* and *The Diary of the Other Health Freak*, both published by Oxford University Press in 2002. If you go onto the **www.teenagehealthfreak.org** website you can catch up with Pete Payne and all his worries about his spots, his girlfriend, his bicycle accidents etc in his day to day diary. Or you can read the books – whichever. And now you, like Pete Payne, can also find out what worries teenagers about relationships all over Britain, and how to get the absolute best answers – by reading this book.

AIDAN MACFARLANE was a consultant paediatrician and public health doctor who ran the child and adolescent health services for Oxfordshire. He is now a freelance international consultant in teenage health.

ANN McPHERSON is a general practitioner with extensive experience of young people and their problems. She is also a lecturer in the Department of Primary Health Care at the University of Oxford.

As well as *The Diary of a Teenage Health Freak* and its sequel *The Diary of the Other Health Freak*, their other books include *Mum I Feel Funny* (which won the Times Education Supplement Information Book Award), *Me and My Mates*, *The Virgin Now Boarding*, and *Fresher Pressure*. They also published a book for parents about the teenage years called *Teenagers: the agony, the ecstasy, the answers*. Their most recent books are *R U a Teenage Health Freak?* and companion volumes to this book on *Drugs*, *Sex* and *Bullying*.

The authors also run the extremely successful website on which this book is based – **www.teenagehealthfreak.org** – which receives around 250,000 hits a week and recently won the BUPA communication award.

Authors' acknowledgements

We would like to thank: all the teenagers who emailed us – whether we were able to answer them or not – and all their parents for having them in the first place. Once again, we would also like to thank Liz and the rest of the team at Baigent for their wonderful work on the website; Mike and Jane O'Regan for all their past support and their funding; Ben Dupré for his continuing patience, sense of humour, and endless excuses on his and our behalf when things get delayed. Cathy Boyd and Becky Mant coded all the emails, which allowed us to identify all those questions on relationships.

Note

The answers we have given to the questions in this book are based on our personal clinical experiences as doctors when dealing with similar clinical problems. Young people reading the book will, we think, be helped by the answers that we have given. However, it is impossible for us to offer advice in such a way as to deal with all aspects of every individual's health problem. Therefore if you, as a reader of this book, have any continuing doubts or concerns about your health problem, we would strongly advise you to consult your own medical practitioner.

To preserve the true flavour of the originals, we have not changed or edited the language or spelling of the emailed questions used in this book. However, in the few cases where real names are used, these have been changed to protect the anonymity of the senders.

relationships

the truth

OXFORD
UNIVERSITY PRESS

Great Clarendon Street, Oxford OX2 6DP

Oxford University Press is a department of the University of Oxford.
It furthers the University's objective of excellence in research, scholarship,
and education by publishing worldwide in

Oxford New York

Auckland Cape Town Dar es Salaam Hong Kong Karachi
Kuala Lumpur Madrid Melbourne Mexico City Nairobi
New Delhi Shanghai Taipei Toronto

With offices in

Argentina Austria Brazil Chile Czech Republic France Greece
Guatemala Hungary Italy Japan Poland Portugal Singapore
South Korea Switzerland Thailand Turkey Ukraine Vietnam

Oxford is a registered trade mark of Oxford University Press
in the UK and in certain other countries

Text copyright © Ann McPherson and Aidan Macfarlane 2004
Illustrations by Tim Kahane 2004

The moral rights of the author have been asserted

Database right Oxford University Press (maker)

First published in 2004

British Library Cataloguing in Publication Data available

ISBN 978-0-19-911231-9

3 5 7 9 10 8 6 4 2

Printed in Great Britain
by Cox & Wyman Ltd., Reading, Berkshire

Third-party website addresses referred to in this publication are
provided by Oxford University Press in good faith and for information
only. Oxford University Press disclaims any responsibility for the material
contained therein.

Contents

All about relationships

Relationships with other people, whether family, friends, lovers or others, are among the most essential things in our lives, and time spent in these relationships can be the happiest moments that we ever experience. But also, sadly, what we may want from relationships is not always what we get, and they can be traumatic and emotionally painful as well. It takes time and patience to learn how to be a good friend and to have good friends and how to be close to other people in your relationships. The way we get good at this is by experience.

It is just as well that, when we set out in life, we don't know all that is going to happen to us, all the friends that we will make and lose, all the relationships that we will build and that will break up. We can, however, all learn from the experiences of what has happened to others – their successes and failures, their pleasures and their pains. That is what this book is all about – how others have managed the relationships and friendships that they have had, what has helped them, what might have helped them even more, and what might help you in your relationships.

By selecting from the more than 80,000 emails that we have now received from young people on the **www.teenagehealthfreak.org** website, we have been able to look at the relationships that young people have – with each other, with adults, with their family and with others. These emails and our answers talk about how these relationships make young people feel, and how they deal with them, how they can overcome problems and how they can improve them.

It's all here for you.

Making friends and
staying friends

Making friends, staying friends and putting limits on friendships are all things that have to be done all the time, at school, out and about and at home. None of these things is ever simple, but it does all get easier as you get more experienced at dealing with relationships.

● TROUBLE MAKING FRIENDS

Dr Dr Ann **I'm really shy at school and I'm moving after summer to a secondary school and I will be splitting up from my friends.** I always find it hard to answer questions in class and make new friends. Got any advice? 14 year old girl.

Dear 'Shy and moving school' – Losing old friends and making new friends is something that we all have to do at different times of our lives, not just when you move schools. Admittedly for some people making friends is easy and it 'just happens' because they have outgoing natures, but most of us are more like you, and it can be more difficult. We have this little shell of shyness and vulnerability that we want to retreat into. So we may have to learn some tricks to help us come out of our shells. Helpful hints include trying to start to talk to people on a subject that you know a lot about. Then try asking someone you want to be friends with about what interests them. Lastly, remember that the person you want to be friends with may be just as shy as you are.

Hi Ann. **I've just started going to school again after six weeks off because of an injury.** I'm finding it really hard to fit in with my friends again 'cause they've made other friends while I was away. I've missed a lot of things that happened. 14 year old girl.

Dear 'Off school for six weeks' – I am so sorry about your hurt, both the injury that kept you off school and now because your friends have found 'new' friends whilst you have been away. I think that people need a certain number of friendships all the time just to feel comfortable with themselves, so that when one friend disappears from their lives – like you did – then they need new friends to take their place. Be patient and keep gently trying to take up your old friendships again. It may take a bit of time, but if they are really friends then they will take you back again.

Dear Dr. Ann, **I am black and don't have any friends as I get picked on by people who don't want to have any thing to do with me coz I am black.** They also think black people take drugs but I have never taken drugs in my life and I would never take them. 15 year old boy.

Dear 'Haven't got any friends coz I am black' – I think what you are finding out about is just how stupid other people can be and the sort of dumb racist assumptions some people make. Don't go along with it though. You will make friends, not least because you don't and won't take drugs, and many, many people will respect you for that. Just be yourself and you will get accepted for the person that you are as long as you stick with it and maintain faith in yourself and your beliefs.

● PROBLEMS WITH FRIENDS

Dear Doctor Ann. **I've always had this thing called cerebral palsy since birth, and I'm in a wheelchair.** I never get to go out with my friends after school cos though everybody's good to me at school they don't want to know afterwards. I feel totally excluded cos they're all going out and doing things together. Boy aged 14.

Dear 'Always had cerebral palsy' – I think that you are going to have to work on your school friends a bit. I know, and you know, and they should know that you are first and foremost just a 14-year-old boy with the same wants, needs and interests as any other 14-year-old – and this includes having good friends who support you all the time – not just at school. So why not explain to them that you want to go out with them and be just like everyone else.

Dear Doctor Ann **I have a good, good friend but I do have a problem with her because I've realised she NEVER apologizes.** I apologize and go along with it all the time. How do I handle it? 16 year old girl.

Dear 'Person with a friend who never apologizes'
– Yes, there are definitely many people around who find it hard to apologize however much in the wrong they are. I think that this is a self-confidence thing. You have to be quite self-confident to be able to say 'I'm sorry, it was my fault' even when that's obviously the case. There is absolutely no need to 'crawl' when doing this even when you are in the wrong, but it does makes life with friends and others infinitely easier if you know how to apologize gracefully. It takes a bit of practice but it is so worthwhile to learn how to do it well! However – be tolerant with your friend as, if it doesn't come naturally, it can be a difficult skill to learn! Perhaps you should try being straight with her. Next time she does something wrong and won't admit it, tell her that you aren't so upset about what she has done but you are really upset that she can't say sorry.

Dear Doctor Ann – **how do you tell a good friend that he can't be trusted?** 15 year old boy.

Dear 'Telling a friend that he can't be trusted' – It sounds as if you have had a bad experience of some kind here. If this is a friend who you have known for some time, you need to sit down and tell him what's bothering you, how you feel and why you feel the way that you do. If, as you suggest, this is a good friendship, then it should be able to withstand the kind of distrust that you have for him at the moment. You need to talk about this to give him a chance to explain whatever it is he's done to make you distrust him like this.

Doctor Ann. **Please help. I'm really worried about a friend of mine who is acting very depressed.** She doesn't talk to me about her problems like she used to and she's much quieter in general. I try to talk to her when she's upset but she says it doesn't matter when it obviously does to her. She hasn't been diagnosed with depression before but I'm really worried. She told me that she

doesn't even think me and her other friends would cry if she killed herself and says she sometimes hates her life. What should I do? I don't want to make things worse as she's not always like this but more than usual now. Worried friend. 14 year old girl.

Dear 'Worried about depressed friend' – I think that you are absolutely right – your friend needs help. When people talk about killing themselves there is a real danger that they might actually try to commit suicide. It sounds as though your friend is depressed but she can be helped, if she can be persuaded to get help. But you shouldn't try to do this all alone. You need help to give your friend help – and you should talk to someone else, preferably an adult, about your worries. I would suggest a teacher at school, your school nurse, or your parents.

Dear Doc. **I get fits when I see lots of zigzag lights and am worried about going clubbing in case the lighting brings on a fit.** My friends don't know I have fits and I'm frightened to tell them in case they stop being my friends. Girl aged 15.

Dear 'I get fits when I see a lot of zigzag lights' – First and foremost I suggest that you tell your friends about your fits – because you are much more likely to scare them away if you suddenly have a fit and they don't know what to do! Many people are terrified when they first see someone having a fit. They even panic and think the person might be dying – which of course they are not! I assume that you are being seen by a specialist doctor (ones that deal with fits are usually called 'neurologists') so as far as going to nightclubs is concerned you should ask him/her about this. What about coming up with other ideas for doing things with your pals – bowling, swimming, shopping etc.

Hello Ann – **I have a problem. I have a friend who I cannot name who has been friends with me since I joined my secondary school.** We get on really well. But these past few months he has changed. He is very rude sometimes and offensive. But most of the time he is ok. I am worried that he is using me. Tomorrow I am going to go out and buy him a present. I fear he will just take the present and leave me. I have been the victim of bullying at my school and my friend has stuck by me. But I am scared I will lose him and I will become a victim. What do I do? My mum tells me that you cannot buy friends. Please help me and reply ASAP. 13 year old boy.

Dear 'Afraid of losing a friend' – Although your mother is absolutely right in saying 'You cannot buy friends', an important part of a friendship is giving each other presents. But normally this is mutual in that you give each other presents, rather than it being just one way. This friend of yours has, in the past, been very supportive of you during hard times, and therefore this friendship obviously means a great deal to you. That fear of losing your friend means that you are giving him signals that you 'need' him as a friend rather than just 'wanting' him as a friend. When people feel 'needed' by other people this can put a strain on any relationship. I think you should relax a bit. Enjoy his friendship when you can, but try to make and enjoy other friendships too. You don't have to put up with him being 'rude and sometimes offensive' to you – maybe finding some new friends would be much better for you!

Dear Doc – **I have this really good friend but this year another girl has started hanging with us.** She's in another class but we have the same maths & German lessons. That's all very well but she hangs around with us all the time and she's really immature. I've spoken to my friend and she feels the same in that we do still wanna hang around with her but just not all the time. Girl aged 14.

Dear 'I have a hanging around friend'
– You touch on a very interesting point about friendship. That is that friendships are not necessarily all or nothing and that there are actually limits to friendship. Sometimes these limits need to be out in the open and discussed between friends. Perhaps you could find ways that you could include this third friend some of the time but not in everything you do. Threesomes can often be difficult, but think how you might feel if you were the third friend...

Getting pressure
2 from friends

Friends can put pressure on you. You might be pressured by your friends in or out of school to do things that you might not otherwise do. We feel this kind of pressure when we go along with things just because we want to be one of the crowd. This pressure can turn into bullying when friends make you feel unwanted because you won't do things their way.

● BULLIED BECAUSE OF YOUR FRIENDS

Dear Ann – **I have a best friend who is totally obese and she is on 'slim fast'.** It is not working for her and she also smells of fish and B.O. She has no friends except me but I am being bullied for

being with her and now even I am finding it hard to be with for the pure stench. At one stage she went very thin on the legs anyway but now she's massive again and has lots of disgusting stretch marks. She doesn't even care how she looks. She insists on wearing tight clothes. I'm so worried and I can't leave her 'cause she will probably kill herself but I can't take her smelling so bad people might think it is me!!!!! Please help. 16 year old girl.

Dear 'Have a best friend who is fat and has B.O.' – Please stick with it as this friend needs you. There are some things you can do to help her with problems such as the B.O. Don't be afraid to talk to her about using anti-perspirants and washing regularly. We all need to do it – but some people simply need to do it more than others! You might need to be more tactful when criticizing her clothes. Why not go shopping for clothes with her and try to encourage her to buy some new things that suit her? She is obviously trying to do something about her weight. Encourage her to eat healthily rather than diet. Maybe you could encourage her to take exercise and even do something, such as swimming, together. There is no quick fix for this but keep trying to help her.

Dear Dr. Ann. **There's this guy in my class who is always getting picked on – I don't really feel sorry for him bcos he brings it on himself.** But he takes out his anger thru violence against his friends who r also my friends too. Now my friends are getting at me because I want to help this guy. What can I do to help them all? 15 year old boy.

Dear 'Wanting to do right by person who is picked on' – You are caught in the middle here and in the end you may not be able to solve

17

everyone's problems completely and make everyone be nice to one another. But don't let these friends, who are picking on this guy, make you into a baddie too. Why are these friends picking on him anyway? Try to find out. You can help the 'picked on boy' by getting him to ignore these bullies as much as he can and not show his anger because by doing this he's only going to make things worse.

● FEELING THE PRESSURE

Dear Doctor, **can u help please? My friend is really worrying me.** Just recently she has become more friendly with a bad crowd. They r older than her. She's 15 and They r 17 and 18. I'm really worried cos they r all in 2 drinking, smoking and do soft drugs. Since she made friends with them she has stopped eating and she keeps fainting. I ask her what's wrong and she just says nothing. Help. 15 year old girl.

Dear 'Good Friend' – Your friend needs help and you're a good friend to want to help her. She seems impressed that this older crowd are taking notice of her and she may also be attracted by the fact that they are into drinking, smoking and drugs. But at 15, she may not be able to handle the pressures that they are putting her under. Keep on being her friend and don't be afraid to tell

her what you think. Also persuade her to see a doctor about the fainting and not eating.

Dear Dr Ann, **a girl offered me a cigarette last week and I said 'no'.** But most of my friends do, so I had 1. At first I thought yugh. But then I thought ok but I have asthma so I know it is really dangerous. But then on the monday after I walked into school and they had weed and they offered it to me but I said 'no'. I know it is illegal. I don't know what to do??? Pleaze help!!!?? Boy aged 14.

Dear 'What to do about offers of cigarettes and weed' – Keep saying yugh, yugh, yugh. I don't really need to tell you about the risks of smoking cigarettes and the same applies to smoking cannabis as it is smoked with tobacco, which is very addictive. That's before going into the other reasons not to take the cannabis – which as you say is still illegal and does have other dangers (including doing your brain in). As you have asthma there is yet another reason not to smoke and cause damage to your lungs. If you find it difficult to say 'no' when you are getting pressure from friends just use your asthma as an excuse.

Dear Dr. Ann, **my friend at school is bullying me coz i am black!** Girl aged 14.

Dear 'Bullied for being black' – Racist bullying is not acceptable under any circumstances. Bullies pick on people who they think are different to them for any reason – because they are black, because they are disabled, because they come from another country, or because they are younger, or cleverer, and so on. You can't count this person as a friend if they are bullying you. Friends defend you from bullying – they don't do the bullying! Tell her how you feel about what she is

doing because there is a chance she might think she is just teasing you. Even so, if it feels like bullying to you be clear to her that it has got to stop.

Dear Doctor, **I am unsure if I am being bullied.** These friends in my class tease me and call me a freak etc because I self harm n was anorexic. When they do something to me though, I sometimes do something back to them. So am I being bullied? 13 year old girl.

Dear 'Being teased for self-harming' – It's bad enough to be coping with self-harming without being teased. Yes, what they are doing is a form of bullying. Your friends may be doing this because they don't know how to react to you hurting yourself and may feel frightened. Try talking to them about it and say how it makes things worse if they tease you.

You might want to talk to one of your better friends or an adult who you trust about the way that you feel. But please, whatever else you do – you should see your doctor or school nurse about your self-harming and find a way to stop it.

3 Friends **forever?**

Although a few friendships may last a lifetime, we also break up with old friends and make new friends all the time. This can be for lots of different reasons – perhaps because we change opinions, change classes or change schools. Sometimes friends simply drift apart and no one is upset, but at other times the parting can be painful and leave us feeling lonely and vulnerable.

● WHEN IS A FRIENDSHIP OVER?

Dear dr. Ann, **my friend at school says that I can't go to a party at his house as I am Chinese and his dad is not allowing me to go.** I think my friend should stand up to his dad if he really is my friend so I don't want to be his friend anymore. Boy aged 14.

> *Dear 'Friend with racist dad'* – It's not your friend's fault that his dad is like this. It is probably impossible, or at least very difficult, for your friend to change his dad's

attitudes at this stage. Your friend has been honest with you about this, and I suspect he feels very badly about it all. Accept his explanation and if you like him, stay his friend.

Dear Dr Ann – **I'm feeling a bit down. I was in a group of friends and we used to go out to someone's house or the cinema almost every weekend.** After a while it seemed that that had stopped happening but a few months later it occurred to me that they hadn't stopped but  that I had stopped being invited and that other people had been going instead, effectively replacing me. Now it's the holidays and while they are all very friendly to me when I talk to them they still keep meeting up without inviting me. I thought of inviting them over to my house to try and remind them but my house is boring and there's not a lot to do. Any ideas? 15 year old boy.

Dear 'Feeling a bit let down' – It's a basic human need to want to feel part of a group. It gives us a huge feeling of security and self-confidence, and we often don't realize how much we need this until we are excluded from the group. This exclusion can be sudden, or more gradual – as you describe. It is certainly not always clear why it has happened, but it may be because the others have 'moved on' in some way. But what should you do about it? Don't hang around on the fringes of the old group feeling sad and begging to be let back in – it just doesn't work that way and it will make you feel bad about yourself. Instead you need to look forward to being included in a new group, and to do that it helps if you make a positive effort to make new friends – to go out and be with new people. You will gradually find yourself surrounded with, and included in, a new group of friends.

Dear Ann, **my best friend has found a new best friend just coz I was off sick for 2 weeks with glandular fever. I feel really lonely. Why did she do it?** Girl aged 15.

Dear 'Best friend has a new best friend' – This might have happened because your old best friend was lonely whilst you were away. That doesn't mean that you can't go back to being best friends with her again but it might mean sharing her as a best friend with her new best friend. You may find that it is actually more fun doing things with three of you together! Try it out and see. I hope that your glandular fever is better now.

GETTING OVER LOST FRIENDS

Ann – **my best girlfriend just dumped me over nothing. I'm so upset. We've been friends for 9 years. What am I going to do?** 15 year old girl.

Dear 'Dumped' – There's no way round this – being dumped by a friend is always painful, tends to make you feel less self-confident and leaves you struggling. This is especially true if the friendship was a long-term one, like yours. But life has to move on and so do you. Very few friendships last a lifetime, and just as you will have to get used to moving from one school to another or one place to another as you get older, you will get used to changing friendships. Changing friends doesn't always mean dumping old friends, but it does mean that we have to find ways of making new friends. You will make new best friends. Until then you have to learn to fall back on yourself and be self-confident enough to trust that better times will come again.

Hi *Doc,* **I've had a bit of a bust-up with one of my friends.** We always go around in a three and it pretty much works except for when the other two have small arguments. Now we've broken up because of a tiny thing. What should I do? 14 year old girl.

Dear 'Had a bit of a bust-up' – Friendships are never the same all of the time. When things are going well, friendships are strong and easy. At other times they are weaker and arguments and disagreements disrupt them. Good friendships usually manage to survive these ups and downs, so keep at it – but be prepared that if things get really bad you may have to let these friends go and find new ones.

Making new
4 friends

Do you worry that you will never have the confidence to go out and meet people who could become a boyfriend or a girlfriend? Do you think that you just won't meet the right person or that if you do you won't know how to make the very first move? You are not alone because lots of people feel like this – but there are things that you can do to help.

● FEARS AND SHYNESS

Hi Doc – I am a Lad of 15 and have never had a girlfriend because I haven't had the guts to ask. Many of my peers get others to do the dreaded asking but I don't think this is right. Have u any hints or tips on how to do it or what I should do? 15 year old boy.

Dear 'Haven't had the guts' – There is a Chinese saying that 'Every thousand mile journey has a first step'. You need to take that first step and once you have taken it, you will find the rest easier. That first step may seem like it's struggling up a mountain – but it isn't. It is as simple as saying to a girl 'Hello, did you see that telly program last night?', 'What did you think of that disco last week?', or 'Do you like the new Norah Jones CD?' Then listen, listen, listen to the reply. Also, remember that the girl may be just as anxious as you about it all – and she will be totally delighted that it was you who made the first move.

Dr Ann – **I'm 16 and haven't had a girlfriend.** The reason was because of my extreme shyness with girls but I've mostly grown out of that. Now the problem is I'm worried all girls have had loads of boyfriends and will either expect too much from me or think I'm sad and not even bother with me. My mates tell me to pretend I have had a few. I know they mean well but they don't realise I don't  want to just pretend. I don't think most girls like a shy boy so I have no hope. Please tell me what I can do. 16 year old boy.

Dear 'Haven't had a girlfriend' – Correct me if I'm wrong, but I think you're defending yourself against rejection with a whole series of different excuses. Nothing wrong in that – we all do it. You feel that you couldn't take someone saying 'No'. You are going to have to take a deep, deep breath and plunge in and find out that it just isn't as bad as you think and that one girl will actually say 'Yes please' if you do ask. Make the leap and once you have you'll wonder what you were so worried about. And by the way – you are right – don't pretend that you have had lots of girlfriends in the past. If anyone asks why you haven't had a girlfriend before, just say it was because you hadn't met the right person to ask out. There's no point in lying – somewhere down the line you will be found out.

Dear Doc. **I can't get a girlfriend. I am too shy to go up to a girl I like and talk to her.** And what if she has a boyfriend or doesn't like me back? Please help. 14 year boy.

Dear 'Too shy' – You can get a girlfriend – just don't rush it. Actually we are all shy in some situations. Just try wandering up to girls who you don't really, really fancy and try saying something to them. If possible give them a compliment – remarking on their clothes is a good thing to start with – because we all like to be flattered. Take it from there. And don't forget – girls are terrified of rejection as well!

WHEN YOU REALLY LACK SELF-CONFIDENCE

Dear Doc – **I feel like a freak because I don't get the same attention as my mates and I feel as though no ladz going to like me even though my mates say they do.** How can I have more confidence in my self??? 14 year old girl.

Dear 'Feel like a freak' – Stop comparing yourself with your mates. You are you – and the ladz are going to like you for what you are – a totally unique, one-off, special person. If you only stop worrying about it and relax a bit they will start coming to you. When they do – please be kind to them – as they may be shy and lack self-confidence themselves.

Dear Ann – **I feel real bad. I can't seem to get a girlfriend. All the girls that I like will have nothing to do with me and the ones that like me are like me – all weird and fat.** That or they are tramps or someone who makes you sick. I feel that I have no hope and it might be better giving up now and becoming a lonely old man. 17 year old boy.

> *Dear 'Feeling real bad'* – I am very, very sorry you feel this way – but you don't have to. Stop seeing yourself as weird and fat, and see yourself as brainy and great – or whatever other good attributes you have. But it does also sound as if you are being a bit arrogant in judging the girls as being 'tramps' or 'someone who makes you sick'. How well have you got to know these girls before you make these judgements? Or are you just dismissing these girls to protect yourself because you are afraid to take things further? Perhaps you should give yourself and them a chance to find out more about each other.

● PRACTICE MAKES PERFECT

Dear Dr Ann **I'm worried I'll never get a g/f. I try 2 be real sensitive and when I do ask them out they laugh in my face what should I do?** Will I ever find the right one? From Lonely Heart. 16 year old boy.

> *Dear 'Lonely Heart'* – Yes, yes, yes – you absolutely will find the right one, but maybe not straight away. You will have to try and try again. I can't really believe that they all laugh in your face. Many girls really like sensitive men, who will listen to them and be aware of their feelings. No one says that it's

easy telling someone how you feel. It does take practice so don't give up. Exposing your own feelings allows the person that you are trying to get to know to more easily reveal their own feelings, but they won't do it until they see that you are willing and able to do it yourself.

Dear Dr Ann, **I really want a boyfriend but I can't find anyone I really like.** I have been asked out by a lot of boys but I don't like any of them. And I am scared of going out with a boy 'cos I haven't been out with a boy before. 14 year girl.

> *Dear 'Really wanting a boyfriend'* – Are you waiting for Mr Right to come along first time round? Actually relationships are not like that. It takes practice to find out what kind of boy suits you and your personality and the only way to find out about that is to experiment a bit by going out with all sorts of different boys. You can have boyfriends who are just friends, boyfriends who you can trust, and boyfriends who you can respect – but it doesn't mean that you have to take things any further unless you want to.

● GOING ABOUT THINGS THE WRONG WAY

Ann – hey! **I'm 15. I've never had a proper boyfriend. It's not that I'm ugly or anything I just don't get asked out.** I've snogged a lot of boys but they seem to think that's all I want when I really want a boyfriend to hang out with. What am I doing wrong? Girl aged 15.

> *Dear 'Snogged a lot of boys'* – You may indeed be going about this in the wrong way. Hold the boys off a bit and make

them work a bit harder for your favours. Boys tend to categorize girls (just as girls may categorize boys) and if you're not careful you're going to be thought of as 'easy'. It's time to change your image. You can remain friendly but also be just a bit more distant until you have sussed out which boy is the right one for you to take things a bit further with – but only when you want to. Snogging is usually more fun if you already have a relationship with the person.

Making the
5 right
moves

So you have met someone you really like and you want to take the next step and begin or develop your relationship. But what happens if you are so shy, embarrassed, unsure of yourself that you have difficulty making the next move – how do you manage it?

● TAKING THE NEXT STEP

Ann – **I am 16 and I have a bit of a problem taking things further with girls.** Don't get me wrong or anything, I am heterosexual and like girls. My friends say it's because I make friends very quickly and that by the time I get round to asking we've become close friends and they say that they don't want to lose our friendship. What should I do? 16 year old boy.

Dear 'Problem with taking things further with girls' – There is this chancy moment in a relationship, which you talk about, where you want to move on from being 'just a friend'. You also point out that sometimes the better friends you are, the more difficult it is to bring up the subject of wanting to become more intimate and for it to develop into a sexual relationship as well. The first thing that you need is a bit of P and Q (peace and quiet) where the two of you are alone – like seeing a film together. The second thing you can do is try to find out how she feels about taking things further by discussing it as if it were someone else involved like 'How would you tell someone that you fancied them a bit more than just being good friends'. See how that goes to start with.

● FINDING OUT IF THEY LIKE YOU TOO

Dear Doctor Ann – **I really like this boy who is my best friend and he knows it. The problem is he don't wanna go out with me cos I aint his type.** Wot am I gonna do? I know this sounds pathetic but I've liked him for almost 2 years. 14 year old girl.

Dear 'Wanting to go out with best friend' – There is so much to relationships – like friendship, the way that you both feel about things and lots else – and then along comes this extra complication that you suddenly fancy the guy something rotten and you want to go further. Are you absolutely sure that you 'aren't his type'? If you get on so well together as best friends then maybe you are but he doesn't know it yet. Be patient about getting closer to him – everyone can change their mind given time. Even if nothing happens, you can at least be pleased that he is a best friend!

Hi there Dr Ann, **I like this friend of mine, a guy I've known since 11 yrs old.** I know him v well but I dun know if he likes me or not. My friend tried to be helpful n asked him if he liked me. He wouldn't answer in a proper way n just says it's a secret. Rumours say that he does. Plz tell me what can I do to find out the truth. Girl aged 17.

Dear 'I like this friend of mine' – Flirtation is the normal beginning of taking a friendship into a boyfriend-girlfriend relationship – but flirtation is a very delicate game. Your friend who is being a 'go-between' might help things, but the guy might feel that she's just being nosey and that he is being pressurized. You might need to make a more direct advance yourself now. If you have known him for six years you must know his likes and dislikes pretty well – music, football team, clothes etc? Try to get him alone and start a conversation about something easy and neutral and then gradually move it in the direction that you want – which is to find out whether he fancies you as much as you fancy him. If he does, he'll find some way of showing it when you are alone, but prepare yourself for the fact that the answer could be 'no'.

● **OVERCOMING FEAR AND EMBARRASSMENT**

Ann – I like this girl a lot and just don't know what to do. I just keep getting embarrassed when I see her and I just don't know how to get started. 14 year old boy.

Dear 'I like this girl a lot' – Making a first step in a relationship can be agony because it means exposing your feelings. The only way out of this is to get in some practice and

to take some risks. Choose a moment when your are alone with this girl as things go much easier when you don't have half your mates around gawping at you and egging you on. Find something good to say about the way she looks, as we all like being complimented. If that first step goes well then you will find that your embarrassment will melt away.

Dear Ann, **there's this guy I really like at school. I think he likes me too because he keeps looking at me. But I don't know whether to ask him out or just leave it.** I'm dying for him to ask me out but what if he doesn't and I ask him out and he doesn't even like me? Please help. 14 year old girl.

> *Dear 'Should I ask him out?'* – Yes definitely. Frequently, at the beginning of a relationship both of you may be shy about taking things further – but it only takes a little step
>
>
>
> forward on your part and then you'll know whether or not he's really interested. Asking him out isn't committing you to anything, after all. I know that we all fear rejection when we expose our feelings to someone else, and it can, and does, make us feel very vulnerable – but it is the same for both of you – so go on, try taking the first step.

Doc, **I really like a lad in the year above me and he knows about me liking him. The trouble is I've never spoken to him and when I**

try I chicken out 'cos I think he'll reject me. Now I've
found out that he likes me how can I get the
confidence to speak to him? Girl aged 15.

*Dear 'Really likes me but worried
he'll reject me'* – You are way, way up
on the game if you know that he likes you – because it's really
unlikely that he will reject you. So where do you go from here?
People usually show that they are attracted to each other by
little glances, touching, laughing at the same things
together – all that kind of thing. For this to happen for you,
you need to be around him a bit more. Any chance of fixing
this, perhaps by asking him to help you with an essay or
something like that?

Dr Ann, **I really fancy this girl but she is in the year below me at
school. I think she may fancy me a bit as well but I want to go
further.** The problem is I am a bit shy when it comes to girls (I
blush etc!) and I was wondering what exactly are the best times
and ways to ask a girl out? Do I ask her personally 1-2-1 or get a
friend to do it or what? Please help! Boy aged 14.

Dear 'I really fancy this girl' – It sounds to
me as if you already have some experience with
girls if you know that you blush when you make
moves on them. You also realize that she fancies
you a bit, which probably means that you have
some other experience of girls fancying you. You
certainly sound enterprising enough to go out on a limb, risk a
bit, and make the first move. Don't leave this to a friend – you
need to do it personally 1-2-1. But if you really can't do that try
going out as a group and take it from there.

● GOING FURTHER

Dear Doc – **me and my boyfriend have been going out for 7 months but we haven't even kissed yet.** We both want to but we're too shy. Everyone says I should make the first move but how? I've never kissed a boy before. 14 year old girl.

Dear 'Wanting to kiss' Most people feel very tentative about making the first move in taking a friendship into a relationship. One way forward is to talk and check out with your boyfriend how he feels about the idea. Or you could wait for the right moment when you are alone together, having a good time, feeling relaxed and happy, and then sort of allow things to happen. Both are good ways and you don't have to rush either of them.

● MOVING FORWARD IN GAY RELATIONSHIPS

Dear Dr. Ann **I quite like this boy and I'm thinking of asking him whether he fancies me but I'm quite shy and I don't know whether he's gay too.** I don't think people believe me when I tell them I'm shy when asking this sort of thing. Please help me and tell me what I should do! 16 year old boy.

Dear 'Shy about being gay' – I can quite understand you feeling a bit shy when asking other boys whether they are gay. Even in our present world where we can talk about sex more freely, it is normal to feel quite tentative about asking other people about their personal sexual feelings. I think that you are going to have to choose the right moment when you and he are alone together. You could then start discussing the subject of people who are sexually attracted to the same sex as themselves without referring to yourself and see what his response is. If he suggests that he might feel the same way – then you can discuss what you want to do. If not, then you can back off, because you are not going to change his feelings.

Dear Ann **I think I may be gay. How do I know and what should I do?** How do I tell my friends who talk about boys all the time? 15 year old girl.

Dear 'I may be gay' – It can be extremely difficult to know whether you are gay or not and frequently it is not an 'all or nothing' kind of thing. Many young people are attracted to people who are the same sex at one time or another. Don't rush into anything yet, whatever your sexual feelings, as you have lots of time to decide, and it does take time to sort these feelings out.

6 Age differences

The older you get the less important a few years difference becomes. There is a big difference between a 3-year-old and a 5-year-old but very little difference between a 22-year-old and a 24-year-old. Girls tend to mature at a younger age than boys, so girls often go out with boys a bit older than themselves. However, when there is a big age difference the worry is that the younger partner may be being persuaded or even forced into doing things that they don't want to do.

● WHEN HE IS OLDER THAN HER

Dear Dr Ann, **I really like this boy at school and I have done for quite a while now.** He is 2 years above me at school and I can understand he wouldn't want anything to do with me but I have met him once on a friday night but not got off with him. The problem is he never calls me. How can I get him to like me? 14 year old girl.

Dear 'Never calls me' – A 16-year-old boy may think that someone aged 14 is too young, or it may be nothing to do with your age. Whatever, this boy is giving you the message that he's not interested. I think you're going to have to accept this. He may well like you, but not want to go out with you. Maybe you could accept just being friends for now and then you never know what might happen in the future.

Hi. **My friend's going out with this 17 yr old boy (she's 14), and I think he's using her. I've talked about this with two other close friends and they agree with me.** They've not had full sex yet but they've done everything else. She decided to wait until she was at least 15 before she has sex with him & he said he'd respect that but then the other day he asked her if using the withdrawal method was ok. She said 'no' but that's what is making me & my friends wonder if he's just trying to get sex off her. Obviously she doesn't see it this way because they're quite close & have been together for half a year but the problem is that we don't know whether to tell her what we think or not as it might hurt her feelings. Do you think we should tell her or just leave it? 14 year old girl.

Dear 'Worried about a friend with an older boyfriend' – Yes, do tell her what you think – that is what good friends are for. Your friend is telling you everything about her relationship with this boy, so she obviously wants your opinion, or at least your approval. If she is happy to talk to you about it, you have the right to make suggestions to her. At least tell her that the withdrawal method is not an O.K. method of contraception. In fact, if she tries this she is putting herself at risk of getting pregnant and getting sexually transmitted infections. Support her in her decision to wait till she's at least 15 before having sex and perhaps suggest that it would be even better to make it legal by waiting till she's 16.

WHEN SHE IS OLDER THAN HIM

Dear Doc – **how do you impress an older girl whose five years older than you?** 13 year old boy.

Dear 'Wanting to impress an older girl' – I doubt that an 18-year-old girl is going to be very interested in a 13-year-old boy. I'm sorry about this but it sounds like you might have a crush on her and she is unlikely to be impressed if you try to show off to her, chat her up or anything else. I suggest that you find someone more your own age to impress!

Dear Doctor Ann **this may sound a bit pointless but I don't know what to do. I like this lad and he likes me. We get along really well and I think we r gonna end up goin out.** The only problem is that he is a year younger than me and a bit shorter as well. I just thought it might b weird goin out wiv some one younger and shorter than me. He is 13 and I am 14. Girl aged 14.

Dear 'Liking a younger, shorter boy' – Stop worrying over nothing – there is nothing wrong about going out with someone a year younger than you. He may be shorter than you because he hasn't had his growth spurt of puberty yet (boys tend to have their puberty a little later than girls). So watch out as you go out with him, as he may suddenly be as tall, if not taller, than you are. But who cares if he doesn't – it's what he's like as a person and how well you get on together that really counts.

● WHEN THE AGE DIFFERENCE IS TOO MUCH

Dear Dr. Ann, **I have been talking to a girl for quite some time now and she really likes me and I like her but there is one small problem. She's only 13 and I'm 17 in a few months.** Would it be wrong to go out with her? Plz help. 17 year old boy.

Dear 'Boy who is developing a relationship with a young girl' – I'm afraid that this is a very unequal relationship. As a 13-year-old girl she will be inclined to rather worship you because you are so much older. But if you are really as mature as your age, then you will realize that this will be more like puppy love on her part. If I were you, I would really, really try very hard to find someone more your own age.

Dear Doctor Ann – **I have just turned 13 but my boyfriend thinks that I am 16. He wants kids and he is 20.** I am scared that he will dump me when I tell him my real age. What shall I do? I wear a gel filled bra to keep up. Help me. Girl aged 13.

Dear 'Lying about your age' – Stop lying now and tell your boyfriend the truth about how old you are. He may dump you and that might be a good thing! It is illegal if he has sex with you until you are at least 16 and the last thing that you should be doing is getting pregnant and having kids now. There is plenty of time for all that stuff when you are older.

How do I know it's 'love'?

7

Telling the difference between 'liking someone a lot', 'wanting sex with someone' and 'loving someone' is difficult and can really only be learnt about through experiencing these different feelings.

● **IS IT LOVE?**

Dear Ann – **what happens when you love someone but they do not know you love them?** Please answer my question it is a matter of help. 13 year old girl.

> *Dear 'Is it possible to love someone without them knowing?'* – Yes it's certainly possible, but how often does this word 'love' actually mean 'fancy' or 'would like to go out with' or 'want a relationship with'? Your feelings may develop into love and love is always better when it is reciprocated. People do talk about walking into a room, seeing someone and instantly falling in love with them, but I'm not sure I would call it love, rather more often it

probably means that they feel a strong physical attraction to them.

Hi Ann, **there's a lad in my form and I've known him for 4 years now. We always flirt with each other and we get on really, really well.** I fancy him and he feels the same about me because we have told each other. I feel differently to him than I do with most lads. I think I love him but I'm really not sure but I know that I've never felt like this towards any other person before. Please help me!! 14 year old girl.

Dear 'I think that I love him' – It sounds like you do feel differently about this boy than others you know, but it probably doesn't really matter whether or not this is love. Only time will tell how this relationship will develop. At 14 you have many years to find out all about what love is and isn't. Love is a whole lot of different things – friendship, loyalty, sexual attraction, respect, trust and affection are a few.

Doctor Ann – hi. **I think I am in love. There is this boy in the year below me at school and even though he isn't the best looking lad I really REALLY fancy him.** My friend told me that he said me and my mate were fit but my mate doesn't care. She has a boyfriend anyway. I really fancy him and my friend told him about this and now he ignores me. I can't stop my self from 'accidentally' turning up in places where he is so I think he thinks I'm stalking him. Also I go to a youth club every week where he goes so I used to talk to him there but I haven't been 4 one reason or another for the last 4 weeks and every time I find out I can't go it gets me down and I cry. What can I do? Please help.

Dear 'Think I am in love' – It sounds to me as though you may be a bit obsessed rather than actually 'in love'. You can only feel love once you have got to know a person really, really well and it does not sound as if you do know this guy at all well yet. So give yourself a chance to get to know some other boys too.

● LOVING TOO MUCH

Dear Doctor Ann, me and my boyfriend have been together for nearly a year and a half and I know it sounds silly but I think I love him too much. I'm only 16 and I don't want to be tied down but I really love him with all my heart. But I'm scared of being without him. Is it possible to be too much in love? Girl aged 16.

Dear 'Think I may love him too much' – Yes, it is possible to be too much in love if it stops you seeing the not-so-good, or even the bad things, about someone. The saying 'love is blind' can be true. It's great that you're happy together but you're right not to want to be tied down yet. It sounds like you are frightened of being without him and may in fact be becoming too dependent on him in this relationship. Keep your other friends. Your love for your boyfriend will be all the stronger for you being independent. Just give yourself time to see how things work out between you. People often look back to a time when they thought they were madly in love with someone and wonder what it was all about.

Dear Doctor Ann – **I've been seeing my girlfriend for a while now. We have a very close and intimate relationship. We see each other all the time. I know she really likes me but the thing is I love her!!** I really love her so much and I don't know how to tell her. I am afraid it might be 2 soon to tell her. I don't want 2 scare her away. And I don't want 2 make a fool of myself if she doesn't like me as much as I like her. Should I wait until I am sure she feels the same way?? Or should I tell her how I feel? Please help as I am really losing sleep over this! 15 year old boy.

Dear 'I love her' – We often worry that our boyfriend or girlfriend doesn't like or love us as much as we like or love them. The best thing to do is relax and be happy that she really likes you and that you get on very well together. Try accepting things as they are. One of the many things about love is that it may not always be totally and perfectly mutual. There are more songs, books, and films about unreturned love than on any other subject. If the other person does not feel the same way there's no way of forcing them to love you. But it does sound to me as if you have a very, very good relationship with this girl – so keep on enjoying it for what it is now.

When to say 'yes'
or 'no' to sex

Most young people don't have sexual intercourse before the age of 16 and many of the ones who do end up wishing they had waited. However, romantic relationships may reach a stage where one or both partners think that having sex might be the next step. Finding out whether it is the right time and whether your partner feels the same way needs to be handled with great care, patience and sensitivity.

● TAKING CONTROL

Dear Ann, **I have a lovely boyf who treats me like a princess. The only trouble is he seems to be obsessed with my breasts!** He always wants to touch them and although I don't mind when we're kissing, he seems to want to do it all the time, even in public. What can I do? I once tried to tell him that it was annoying me but he just started to talk about other stuff (maybe he did not hear me). I love him a lot and I don't mind him touching me in certain circumstances but I feel he is rushing it. Girl aged 15.

Dear 'Treated like a princess' – Even the most wonderful of boys needs to know that there are things which are just not acceptable. You say that you have tried telling him about the way that you feel. By the sound of it he used 'selective deafness' and chose not to hear what he didn't want to hear. Even if you love him, you're going to have to tell him about the way that you feel loudly and clearly. Start with something positive so that his ego doesn't suffer too badly. Something like 'I do love and adore you but... if we're going to continue together there are some times when you are just going to have to control yourself, and respect my needs as well'. I have a feeling that he will actually totally go along with this if he treats you like a princess the rest of the time.

● SCARED HE MAY WANT SEX

Dear Dr, **I'm 14 and I really like this boy. I have liked him for three years now. The other day he asked me back to his house but I'm scared that he just wants me for sex!** Please reply as I need help. 14 year old girl.

Dear 'Scared he just wants me for sex' – Just because a boy asks you back to his house doesn't necessarily mean that it's for sex. But having said that you're being very sensible to question what his motives actually are. You need to discuss this with him before doing anything else. Let him know what you are about and that you are not prepared to have sex with him. As long as he totally understands that then you should be able to go without being scared. Find out who else will be in the house and only go back if an adult is there.

Dear Doc, I have liked this lad for ages at school and we keep making jokes about having sex but I really want to do it and I think he does too. How do we know if we are ready? 16 year old girl.

Dear 'Really want to do it' – As you get older, in most boyfriend/girlfriend relationships there comes a moment when it seems entirely  natural to take things further and to have sex. But it often takes quite a long time for both partners to reach the same point and neither one of you should be rushed into it. It is a moment that is reached via a very 'touchy feely' way forward. As you suggest, sometimes we make jokes about it as a safe way of testing the water without revealing too much. Maybe you now need to stop joking about it and talk seriously to one another about your feelings and make sure that you do both feel the same way. Make sex something special and part of a really good relationship. Before doing anything make sure you sort out good safe contraception to stop you getting pregnant or catching sexually transmitted infections.

Doctor Ann – I've been going out with my girlfriend for two weeks and I feel like I've known her for a lifetime. I think I'm ready to lose my virginity to her but I'm not sure! HELP! Boy aged 15.

Dear 'Ready to lose your virginity' – Isn't this being very rushed and selfish on your part? How about your girlfriend's feelings about all this – have you even talked to her about it? Two weeks is a very, very short time in any relationship – even if you don't think so! Slow down. Have you really reached a stage together where you can talk about your most intimate feelings? Sex is something that should only happen when both people feel it is right for them – without any pressure being put on them.

● YOU DON'T HAVE TO RUSH IT

Dear Doctor – **I'm really upset because my girlfriend won't have sex with me'.** Boy aged 15.

Dear 'Upset because GF won't have sex with you' – Why should what you want be more important than what your girlfriend wants? Back off and make sure that you are not bullying her. Have you listened to her feelings about this? Relationships are built on respecting each other's needs and wants, and it sounds as if you are being a bit selfish and are considering only yourself. Just because your girlfriend doesn't want to have sex with you yet doesn't mean she doesn't like you or that she is rejecting you, it's just that she doesn't think that she is ready. Don't be upset – admire her strength of character and remember maybe she also wants to keep it legal – and it's illegal until she's 16.

Hi. **I've been with my boyfriend for nearly a year now. He's not a virgin. He's had sex twice but hasn't done it with me. Is there something wrong with me?** I've told him I want to have sex with him but he just avoids the conversation. What do I do? 14 year old girl.

Dear 'Wanting sex with your boyfriend' – Be pleased that your boyfriend really respects you and does not want to just have sex with you but wants a proper relationship. It might be that he regrets having sex in the past and feels it is better to wait – especially as you are under the legal age for having sex anyway. Don't push the sex side of your relationship. There's plenty of time and there are lots of other loving things you can do together without actually having sexual intercourse. Most girls of 15 have not had sex, and those that have often regret it.

• PROBLEMS ONCE YOU HAVE STARTED

Dear Ann, **I used to have a great sex life with my boyfriend but now I just don't want that anymore. I just want to hang out with him.** Does this mean I don't love him anymore or is it time to change fellas? 17 year old girl.

Dear 'Just don't want sex anymore' – Even in the best and most steady of relationships, one or other of the partners may go through periods when they don't want to have sex. This may be to do with hormones, sadness, depression or many other things. This is entirely normal and good relationships should be able to withstand these 'on' and 'off' periods of sexual desire. You need to talk to your boyfriend about this because people can feel rejected by their partner not wanting to have sex with them. But don't be afraid to discuss it because he can't be expected to guess about the way that you feel. Give it time. Your sexual desire for him may come back, or it may be that the relationship has changed so that in future you become just friends.

Doc – **I've just become 16 and I have slept with 2 boys. The first time I didn't use anything and the 2nd we did. I've been really drunk both times and both the lads are just mates with me!** I never thought I'd have sex at 16 years old but I had it twice! I slept with one lad 2 weeks ago and 2moro night we are all going out 4 a meal 4 my birthday. Will he expect it again?? All his friends know and I think I'll do it again. I really like him but he only wants one thing. Why can't I find a nice lad that'll love me? 16 year old girl.

Dear 'I've slept with 2 boys but why can't I find a nice lad that'll love me?' – First, for goodness sake stop getting drunk and sleeping with these boys, particularly without using proper contraception (condoms or 'the pill'). Sex is not a substitute for love and sleeping around is going to get you a bad reputation for being 'easy'. That is certainly not going to help you find 'a nice lad who will love you'. Yes, the guy who you have slept with before will probably expect you to sleep with him again, but that doesn't mean that you have to do it. You have a mind of your own and if you don't want to then say 'no' and stick to it.

9 Choosing or **cheating**

In boyfriend/girlfriend relationships, there are times when you may have to choose whether you are going to continue in the relationship, change to another one or cheat and try to run both. But cheating can be very painful for everyone concerned and is rarely a solution.

● CHOOSING BETWEEN THEM

Dear Doc, two year sevens fancy me and they're both best mates. I fancy one of them but I like the other one as a friend. How do I go out with one but not make the other one feel bad because I'm going out with her mate? Please help, its driving me nuts!!!!! Boy aged 14.

Dear 'Being driven nuts' – There is no easy way through this! The best thing to do is be totally honest and explain how you

feel – to both of them. Talk it through, tell them how you feel about each of them and then see how they both feel about you. One may be happy to just continue as your friend and the other may choose to be more than just a friend. You are going to have to take the plunge and find out.

Dr. Ann – **I have this best mate and she has 3 older sisters. The thing is I have secretly been out with one of them and I think she wants to carry it on but I don't know if I can because the one who is my mate would never speak to me again.** Boy aged 16.

Dear 'Carrying on with best mate's sister' – You are not going to be able to continue to 'go out secretly' with your best mate's sister without her finding out – that is for sure. It may be fun carrying on with one of them secretly without the other knowing, but you may lose everything here – your friendship with one and a relationship with the other. So it's decision time. Ask yourself what you want from this and how much the secrecy of your relationship with your best mate's sister is what makes her so attractive to you. If you want to continue the relationship with the sister it might be best to sit down and explain your worries to your best mate first.

Ann, **I have a boyfriend and I went to a festival and kinda got close to another boy other than my boyfriend.** I don't think we did anything and now I'm even more stuck because this other boy, who fancies me, is coming onto me!!! Wot do I do?????? I'm confused. 16 year old girl.

Dear 'Kinda got close to this other boy' – O.K. so most human beings can fancy more than one person at a time. The BIG question is – what do you do about it? There are people around who like to try to pretend that just because you don't actually have sexual intercourse with someone else then you haven't cheated on your partner. But most of us think that if our partner goes off and snogs or rolls around in bed with someone else, even with their clothes on, they have been cheating. So let's be clear about what you mean by 'I don't think anything happened' – either something happened or it didn't. You are simply going to have to stop sitting on the fence and decide between the two of them, though that doesn't mean it will be easy, nor does it mean that choice will be forever.

Dear dr. Ann – **I fancy this boy but my friend goes out with him.** I really, really like him. I feel like battering the girl because she rubs it in my face. I know I shouldn't – what do I do? HELP! 13 year old girl.

Dear 'Fancying friend's boyfriend' – Perhaps your friend doesn't know you fancy her boyfriend. It would be hard for her to be sympathetic even if she did. You need to realize that although you fancy your friend's boyfriend, you should not try to take this any further. One way to stop this hurting so much is to get out and find a guy of your own.

● THE FEAR OF BEING CHEATED ON

Dear Dr Ann – **my best friend just told me that she really fancies my boyfriend that she doesn't know I'm going out with – yet.** What can I do? 14 year old girl.

Dear 'Best friend fancies your boyfriend' – Just because your best friend fancies your boyfriend doesn't mean she plans to do anything about it. She doesn't have to try dating him. You need to tell her now that he is your boyfriend and that you are going out with him. Make sure you explain that all this happened before you knew she liked him. Once she knows this I'm sure she'll back off and leave him to you.

Dear Ann, **I am worried. I am very paranoid about my bf.** I am 16 and get jealous very easy even though I know he loves me and ain't cheating on me – I still think that he might. Please help. Why am I feeling this way? thanks. A 16 year old girl.

Dear 'Jealous' – I would not call you paranoid but normal. Almost all of us go through periods of feeling less or more self-confident. Sometimes it's because of our hormones (like when we have our periods); sometimes it is because other things in our lives are going wrong – schoolwork, losing other friends, for example – and sometimes there is no obvious reason. Talk to your boyfriend about these feelings and explain to him that it isn't that you actually feel he is cheating on you, but rather that you are feeling insecure at the moment and need a bit of extra holding, hugging and reassurance. One of the greatest problems about relationships is that we believe that our partners should be sensitive enough to understand the way that we feel without us having to tell them. It just doesn't always happen this way and to make relationships work we need to explain our feelings to our partners and ask for help when we need it. It is not a sign of weakness to do this and it also allows our partners to do the same when they are feeling insecure.

Dear Ann – **I met this boy at a friend's party. I really fancied him and I know he fancied me!** I've never had a boyfriend before and I would really like to be his girlfriend. The trouble is I've found out that he is a womaniser and would dump me when I lose my virginity to him. What should I do? 16 year old girl.

Dear 'Fancying a womaniser' – Why, oh why are so many girls and women attracted to the 'bad boys'. Is it because these guys know that they are attractive and take advantage of this to seduce as many women as they can? There is a type of addiction to doing this amongst some boys and men – a sort of 'I can and therefore I will' attitude. On the other hand, there are also some women who feel that they can make these boys change their ways. A great idea – which normally just does not work – as I think you already realize! If the boy really fancies

you, as you say, then make him work for you. Play really, really hard to get. If this relationship with him is going to work and he isn't going to just use you, you have to find out whether there can be something serious between you. If he makes the effort over a long time, perhaps you could have a proper relationship with him. But why risk it? He sounds like trouble and you can do better. Walk away from him now and you'll avoid getting hurt and be available if a better guy comes along!

Dear Dr Ann – **my boyfriend is going on holiday for 7 and a 1/2 weeks and I'm scared he will meet someone else and sleep with her and forget about me.** What should I do? 15 year old girl.

> *Dear 'Scared he will meet someone else'* – Trust is an essential aspect of any relationship but a very difficult one! You are going to have to let him go on this holiday because being over-possessive of someone destroys relationships faster than almost anything else. Try to stop worrying and get on with your own life whilst he is away. Deal with your worries when he gets back by talking to him (and listening carefully) to what happened when he was away. The chances are that he will have been faithful to you and both he and you will feel good that you trusted him.

● **WHEN SOMEONE CHEATS ON YOU**

Dr Ann – **my boyfriend is cheating on me and he doesn't know that I know.** What shall I do? 14 year old girl.

> *Dear 'Being cheated on'* – There is only one thing to do and that is to tell him that you know and that you won't tolerate it and that he has to make up his mind one way or the other. He will probably make endless excuses and say that it is really you that he loves and that the other

girl means nothing to him and it was just a passing thing! Judge him not on what he says, but on what he does. If you think that he is going to continue cheating on you, or he does go on cheating on you, then chuck him. Don't be afraid to do this, as there will be lots of other boys to choose from.

10 Arguments, being dropped and breaking up

Many boyfriend/girlfriend relationships have to end somewhere, sometime, somehow. There is no ideal way of managing a break-up – just better ways and worse ways. Here are some of the problems people face when a relationship falls apart.

● WHEN IT'S YOU DOING THE DUMPING

Doc – **I've been seeing this boy for a few months now. He liked me at first & he really likes me still.** He tells me all the time and says I'm perfect. But I don't feel the same! I like him a lot but I sometimes feel weird. I have my eye on someone else but I can't hurt him like that. Please help me. Girl aged 15.

Dear 'Got your eye on someone else' – None of us is perfect but you will be very imperfect if you pretend that you want to be with this boy who 'really likes you'. Are you just staying with him until that someone else gets interested in you? You must tell your current boyfriend that you don't like him as much as he thinks you do. It may hurt him but it's better that he knows the truth as he'll find out sooner or later and it will hurt him even more if you let this go on. There is nothing worse than finding out that you are being taken for a ride when you imagined everything was fine.

FINDING IT HARD TO LET GO

Hi – well I was going out with my boyfriend who is 16 for a year. He lives in West London and I live in Nottingham the thing is he didn't think about the distance until now and he's just finished me because of that. I really love him and he just wants to be friends but I don't know what to say to get him back. Please help. 15 year old girl.

Dear 'Person with long-distance ex' – The distance may not be the only reason that your boyfriend has finished with you, although keeping a relationship going when you are far apart can be very difficult. This boy may find he is starting to enjoy being independent and unattached again. It doesn't sound as though he wants to be tied down anymore and at 16 that's probably a good idea. It's great that he wants to be friends with you, but I don't think – whatever you say – that you'll be able to get him back.

61

Dear Doctor Ann, **I have been with my boyfriend for 9 months now and he has been with other girls behind my back before but always coming back telling me I am the one he loves.** Lately we have both been going off of each other and have decided to split up. He is with someone else now but she is known as a slag. I haven't had sex with him and I think that he has gone out with her just for sex. Do you think that he will come back or is it for good now? Also, my mum does not like him so I have to go out with him as a secret even if he does come back. I don't know if I should say 'yes'. 15 year old girl.

Dear 'Shall I say yes' – I think that you should say 'no', not 'yes'. I think that you really know that that is what you should be saying. Having sex with this boy will not make this relationship work, even if he does try to come back. Why not stay split up and be friends rather than anything else? Why would you want to go out with someone who is only interested in sex, anyway? Your mum is probably right not to like him and the other good thing about saying 'no' to him is that you won't have to keep any nasty secrets from her.

• WHAT TO DO WHEN THERE IS NO HOPE

Hi doc – **I'm feeling really depressed as 3 weeks ago my boyfriend dumped me. We got along so well and always used 2 tell each other we loved each other.** Then out of the blue he finished with me. I was so upset and I still love him even though he has a new girlfriend. I cry all the time and think about him 24/7. We are still like best m8s and see each other all the time as he's in all my classes at school and his new girlfriend gos 2 a different school. I just really want him bk and don't know what 2 do. Do you think there is hope in the future as he does still flirt with me and says he still thinks I'm fit??? 14 year old girl.

Dear 'Dumped' – It is always difficult to get over being dumped, especially if you see the dumper every day. He is not being a best mate to you if he is still flirting with you, even if it makes his own ego feel good. The first time you get dumped is not necessarily the worst but it is definitely nasty. Your pride gets hurt, you feel rejected and you feel that you may never have a relationship again – but you will! Ignore his flirting and go out with other friends. It may make him feel jealous – but it sounds as if it was the right time for you and he to stop being girlfriend and boyfriend. Unfortunately, it may have taken you longer to realize this than him.

● DEALING WITH THREATS

Dear Dr. Ann, **my girlfriend has said that if we ever split she will commit suicide.** What shall I do? 15 year old boy.

Dear 'Worried about splitting' – I am sorry that your girlfriend is making these sorts of threats. This is no reason

to remain in a relationship. If you feel that the relationship is not right, of course you must split. If you think she is serious about the threat of suicide please tell an adult you trust and get her some help. But she may be just trying to make you feel guilty and that is not a good basis for carrying on a relationship with her.

Ex-boyfriends and ex-girlfriends

When relationships are over not only can the sadness linger on, but also your feelings can be very confused about how to behave towards the ex.

● WHEN THE FEELINGS GO ON

Dear Dr Ann – **although I ended the relationship I can't stop thinking about my ex girlfriend.** Please help – boy aged 15.

Dear 'Can't stop thinking about ex-girlfriend' – I'm not sure why your relationship broke up but there was probably a good reason for you finishing it. You may have genuine regrets and there must have been good things about this girl for you to want her to be your girlfriend in the first place. But thinking about her all the time because things

haven't worked out as well as you expected since you split up, doesn't mean it would be right to have her back. It may be that you are now seeing your ex through rose-tinted spectacles – remembering only the good times rather than the bad. Try making a list of the good and the bad things and be realistic about why you finished it. Only allow yourself to think about your ex-girlfriend for 15 minutes a day and then gradually reduce this to 10 minutes a day and then to 1 minute until you are not thinking about her at all. Then get busy seeing other friends, making new friends and getting a new life.

Dear Dr Ann – **what's the best way to forget about some one you fancy or you have been out with?** 15 year old boy.

Dear 'How to forget' – There's no easy way to do this. Different people try different things. It's good to keep busy with other friends, take up a new interest or activity, such as sport, drama or something else. Make a list of all the things you like doing and arrange to do something each day so you don't have time to sit around and mope. You'll soon meet someone else you fancy just as much or even more, but don't throw yourself into another relationship too quickly.

● SEX AND THE EX

Dear Doc – **one of my ex's wants me back but only for sex. He doesn't want to go out with me.** He just wants to 'have some fun'. I kinda feel the same way but should I still go ahead with the 'no strings attached sex?' 16 year old girl.

Dear 'Only for sex' – Say no, no, no, to sex with 'no strings attached'. You may think this is old-fashioned but I still think sex is special and only really fun when there are strings attached and the people involved do care about each other. This kind of relationship always gets complicated because one person usually gets more involved, wants more from the other person and eventually someone does get hurt. The fact that you only 'kinda' feel the same way makes me wonder if you really hope that your ex will in fact stop being an ex and start being your boyfriend again if you give in to him. Don't be fooled!

Hello Dr Ann **I am in a difficult situation. I split with this boy a little while ago. I had sex with him twice. I went out with him 3 times in total and now I am with his best friend who I do not have the same feelings for.** I am not at all sexually active at this moment but I want to get back with my ex. I would do anything to be with him as he said he would like to be with me. Now I do not know what to do nor how to tell my present boyfriend about the feelings I have for my ex/his best friend. Please help me. 15 year old girl.

Dear 'In a difficult situation' – You are in a difficult situation for lots of reasons. You're going to have to face up to what is going on or you will ruin your relationships with these two boys and the friendship between your ex and his best mate. You're messing with these boys' emotions as well as your own. I would suggest you stop going out with anyone for a bit and take some time to sort things out in your own head. At your age it's illegal to have sex with anyone and it's a really bad idea to have sex with someone when you've only been out with them once. Wait and take the time to develop a proper relationship with a boy over months before you make this move. Don't just do it after one meeting, you'll only regret being casual about something that's special.

● GET SORTED – HAVE A BREAK

Dear Doc – I have just recently got off with a lad that I hardly know but I have fancied for ages. I don't feel right when I am out with him but a week ago my ex-boyfriend told me he still had feelings for me and asked me if I was single and this made me think about my relationship with my current boyfriend. But tonight I finished with my current boyfriend but I don't know whether I have done the right thing and I feel really guilty because I have only been with him 2 weeks. What should I do? Please can you give me some advice. 15 year old girl.

Dear 'In a muddle over boyfriends' – It sounds as if neither of these boys is right for you. There may well be things you like about both of them, but not enough to have either of them as a steady boyfriend. It's good that you finished this new relationship quickly and didn't let your new boyfriend think you were really interested when you weren't. You need a break without a boyfriend for a bit until you sort out who you are yourself and what you want from a relationship before getting involved again.

Internet relationships

With the arrival of the internet came internet relationships. Wherever and whenever teenagers talk to one another, relationships spring up. But the internet has special dangers for people wanting to find a relationship because you don't always know who you are talking to, how old they really are or what the other person really wants.

● **DANGERS**

Hi – my problem is this guy. I met him on the net. I emailed him a couple of times and he's emailed me quite a few times last week. He is 14 and kept coming on and off line on the net and then he said to me that he couldn't let go. When I said why? he sed that he couldn't leave me all alone on the net. He emailed me 4 times in one day. He emails me just to say 'hi'. He once emailed me from the phone box saying hi and could we meet. I want him to be straight with me. What do you think I should do?????? Please help me. Thank you. 13 year old girl.

KeepOut

Dear 'Met on the net' – Do not take this any further. You have no idea how old this 'guy' really is. Older men (really, really old – 30, 40, 50 years old or even more) have become experts at using the internet to persuade young girls like yourself to meet them. It is called 'grooming' and has just been made a criminal offence by the government. These men pretend to be the same sort of age as the callers they meet in chat rooms (say, 14 years old) and may even send a photo of a young boy and pretend that is a picture of themselves just to persuade you to meet them. This is very, very dangerous. You have no way of knowing the actual truth about this person, however serious and honest they appear to be. So don't be fooled or be foolish. End this 'net relationship' now and find someone your own age who you actually know from school, or from meeting through your friends or family – as long as you know them personally and NOT from the net.

Dear Ann – **I have a problem with some boys I know. I met some boys off the internet and I have kept in contact with them for a long time.** Except I have become close to all three of them. They all say 'I love you' and I like them all A LOT. I even think I love one of them. Or maybe two. I don't know how to tell them and if I do I might hurt one of them. What shall I do? Girl aged 14.

NO ENTRY

Dear 'Having problems choosing between boys you met on the net' – Relationships formed on the internet can feel like something very intimate over a short period of time without you really knowing how true anything is about the people that you are revealing yourself to. You may think that you know them, and they may think that they know you, but how can this be? And how can these three boys really say they 'love' you? Love is a very complex emotion made up of many, many different things – such as trust, respect, friendship, and affection – that are built up over time. It's hard to see that true love can develop between people who have never met. A hundred years ago, people used to fall 'in love' with one another by exchanging letters over a period of time, but many of these 'pen relationships' were actually a disaster when the people met face to face! If you did decide to meet then you will need to be very, very careful indeed, and make sure that you take someone with you because these boys may not be boys at all, but may actually be older men.

● NET EMOTIONAL BLACKMAIL

Dear Ann, **I got talking to this boy on the internet and he asked if we cud start going out, which I said 'yes' to but didn't take at all seriously cuz its over the internet.** We've been talking for about 6 months now and I've talked to him over the fone a lot and he seems ok. But he sez if I ever left him he would kill himself. He wants to meet me which I'm ok about and I'll make sure its safe etc. But I don't know what to do. I don't want a relationship with him and if I tell him he's going to do something stupid. Please help me cuz i have no idea wot to do!! 15 year old girl.

Dear 'Got talking to this boy on the internet' – Do you really, really know anything at all about this boy except what he has told you on the internet? How do you know he is

not lying through his teeth? How can he say to you that he would kill himself if you left him when you haven't even met each other? That is just emotional blackmail and it sounds like he could be a great danger to you. You say that he wants to meet you and you are O.K. about this and will make sure it's safe etc – but how are you actually going to do that? I very strongly suggest that you don't meet up with him. However, if you do you must make sure it's in a very, very public place like a café that you know. Also, take some friends with you and tell him ahead of time that they will be with you. Stick to your guns about this even if he tries to persuade you otherwise. I hate to be cynical but I'm afraid it is very likely that this is just an older guy who is conning you and it would be stupid to meet up with him. Even if he's genuine, there is absolutely no reason for agreeing to meet this guy in the first place if you have no intention of having a relationship with him.

● BEING UNFAITHFUL ON THE INTERNET

Hi Ann! I really, really need some advice and have nobody to talk to :(. About 3 months ago I met this guy on the internet. He's really nice. We understand each other completely and can relate to each others problems. It's amazing – like we're connected. We're soul mates :) . Anyway he is actually 'going out' with this other friend of mine who I've known for about 4 years now and they see each other all the time. Thing is they really love each other and I feel so left out. He's the only person who I can talk to about my problems 'cos I feel nobody else understands or even cares – but it is just the internet between

us. I'm so attached to him I think I'm in love with him :(. It really hurts 'cos he talks to me as if he loves me and tells me how much he cares about me and how much he wants to hold me and kiss me. But he has this other girlfriend who happens to be one of my best friends!! He says he thinks about me all the time. I know I think about him all the time. I'm obsessed with him. We're going to meet for the first time separately from my girlfriend soon but I don't know what I'm going to do. He wants us to go and see his girlfriend but I can't deal with seeing them kissing and cuddling and telling each other how much they love each other :(. I logged into his email the other day I don't know why :(. He gave me his password. I had to look and went thru all the mail he's sent his girlfriend. I was so hurt. He talks to her exactly how he talks to me but with a few 'I love yous' here and there :(. I read them all over and over like I wanted to hurt myself. I wanted to see what he's been saying to her :(. So anyway this really upset me so I cut myself. I started cutting myself about a year ago but recently he got me out of it with his advice. Knowing he's there for me and he cares really helped. But I was just so upset and my life seemed so crap and hopeless I had to do it. I know it was wrong but... it's too late now :(. D'oh! Please try your best to help me Dr Ann. If I talk to him about this then I'll lose our friendship because we can't be friends if I love him. I don't want to lose our friendship. It's the most amazing one ever but I can't carry on like this. Damn I love him :(. From Love sick puppy. Girl aged 15.

Dear 'Lovesick puppy' – This guy is being unfaithful to your friend via his internet relationship with you. How would you like it if he were going out with you, but at the same time emailing your best friend and saying that he loved her? You are going to have to find a way of finishing this relationship now – for your own sake. You need to go out and find someone who isn't attached to someone else – someone for yourself who you can really be intimate with, rather than just swap emails with. Intimacy itself is about so much more than swapping secrets by email (though this can certainly be part of a relationship!). Rather than trying to lure this guy away from your friend, why not wish them well with their relationship together and find another friend of your own.

Teacher
troubles

13

Teachers are there to help and support you whilst you are at school. They can be good friends but they can never, ever be more than that, even if you find yourself fancying your favourite teacher. Occasionally a teacher does overstep the mark, but the punishments for this are very severe.

● **TEACHERS AND FRIENDSHIP**

Hi Ann, I don't know if I'm normal. There's this teacher at school and I really like her, like she's my friend and I feel I can tell her everything and she's like my second mum. Is this normal? Girl aged 14.

Dear 'Don't know if liking teacher is normal' – Not only are you perfectly normal, you're also very lucky to have a teacher as a friend to whom you can tell everything. In fact it is a very, very good thing for any young person to have a close friend outside their family (as well as inside the family) who they can tell 'everything to'. It helps stop young people from getting into all sorts of trouble – like taking drugs or missing school. If I could prescribe 'having a teacher as a good friend' to all the students that I see in my medical practice – I definitely would.

Dear Dr Ann. **I have got a really big crush on a male teacher at our school he is about 29 and I dream about him all the time.** I blush when he passes me and I really like him and want to tell him. What should I do? Girl aged 14.

Dear 'I have a really big crush on a male teacher' – There is nothing wrong with you having these kinds of feelings. But you are going to have to learn to admire and like someone without actually fancying them or having a crush on them. Teachers are in a position of absolute responsibility for you and cannot and will not respond to your feelings. So my advice to you is to keep on blushing but **DEFINITELY DO NOT DO ANYTHING ABOUT IT.** All your teacher would do if you tell him (if he is nice about it) is explain that he is your teacher and absolutely nothing more.

Dear Doctor Ann – **I fancy a P.E. teacher at my school. I really love her. What should I do?** 14 year old boy.

Dear 'Fancying your P.E. teacher' – You may fancy your teacher, but I'm sure that you don't love her. Many boys and girls fancy their teachers at one time or another and this is not surprising. Teachers can be attractive people and they are in a powerful position at school and that makes them appealing to young people. Also, at around the ages of 9 to 16, young people are going through puberty when their sex hormones are beginning to affect both their bodies and brains and this greatly increases their interest in love and sex generally. But, but, but – teachers cannot and should not have any kind of relationship with a student other than a normal student–teacher one. A teacher can be your friend, but they definitely cannot be more than that. So the answer to your question 'What should I do?' is – go out and make friends with girls more your own age.

● ABSOLUTE NO-NOS

Dear Doc – **help! There is this teacher and I quite fancy him and he is really coming on to me.** I know he's married but he's asked me out to lunch alone with him and I don't know what do. Girl aged 16.

Dear 'Teacher is really coming on to you' – I do understand your confusion because it can be quite flattering to have this attention from your teacher. We all like to be appreciated, even when it is by someone who we know should not be doing it. This is a very difficult situation for you to deal with, and I don't think that you should be trying to deal with it alone. You need to tell someone about it. Tell your parents if you can, but I do understand that you might find this difficult. Telling another teacher that you can trust might be preferable for you, or another adult friend. Meanwhile – DO NOT go out to lunch with him. Put it off and find someone who can help you. This absolutely should not go any further.

Dear Dr Ann **I think my teacher likes me. He always watches me in his lessons.** Please help. 14 year old boy.

Dear 'I think my teacher likes me' – O.K. so your teacher likes you – but that is probably all there is to it. Don't start fantasizing that it is anything more than that. It may be that he is just making sure that you are paying attention. If anything else does actually happen, like he asks you out after school, then you must absolutely say 'no' and tell your parents about it immediately.

Getting on
with parents

14

Getting it right with your parents gets more and more complicated as you get older. One moment you want them to be looking after you, caring for you and making sure that you are all right. The next moment you want them to leave you alone and let you get on and do what you want to do.

● **CAN'T TALK TO YOUR PARENTS?**

Dear doctor, **what do I do? My mum doesn't know I'm going out with this boy and I'm afraid she will go spare because he's 19.** All my friends know and I want my mum to know but she'll flip. He hasn't asked for sex. He really cares for me so why should she have a problem? 16 year old girl.

Dear 'Mum doesn't know about older boyfriend' – I think you really do want your mum to know so why not tell her? It's much easier than trying to hide it or lie to her, especially as mums have a nasty way of guessing what's going on anyway. Your mum is most likely to flip if she finds out you have been deceiving her. The reason she will be worried about the age difference is because she might feel that you're being pressured into having sex or doing things you don't want to do. Explain that this hasn't happened and reassure her that you know there's no need to have sex with him even if he asks for it. If she realizes you have a mature attitude about this she might feel better.

Dear Doc, **my mom thinks I'm all naive n pple can get into my head easy. That it's easy for pple to (peer) pressure me into things.** The reason she thinks this is b/c she doesn't know me for me. She works full time n the only time I see her (in morning n night) she is yelling at me b/c she lets out all her anger at me. I understand that she doesn't know how to deal with her anger so she lets it out on me but i mean she doesn't even know me so how can she judge me? what can I do how can i get through to her? Please help! 16 year old girl.

Dear 'Daughter of hard-working mother' – **You two need to sit down together and talk about what is going on. Many mothers (and fathers) have to work full-time but that is not an excuse for her not understanding you. Part of her anger may be that she is actually cross with herself. She may feel guilty that she is not spending enough time with you and worried because she doesn't really understand what is going on with you and she is probably imagining the worst. Find out what she thinks that you are up to, tell her what you are really doing and start getting in contact with one another in a more realistic way. This is going to take time but you are mature enough to book a time together and start talking calmly and sensibly about this.**

Dear Ann – **I'm forever going out with lads but can never tell my family cos I'm afraid of what they'd say.** I went to a club recently and got off with lads and my friends get mad with me for keeping it secret from my parents. Wot can I do? It really upsets me that I can't be open. 16 year old girl.

Dear 'I never tell my family what I do' – You may be unable to tell your family about what is going on because you know they won't like it. This may be because they are very strict or it sounds more likely that it's because you don't really approve of what you are doing yourself. If your friends are getting mad at you, think again – maybe they think what you're doing is wrong too. Please listen to your friends even if you won't listen to your family.

Hi Doctor Ann. **I am a black-african girl and in our tradition a girl should not talk to her parents about any issue involving sex.** The problem is I have been in the UK for more than 3 yrs with my parents and i feel quite close to my mother. I am still a virgin but I intend on having sex with my boyfriend who is 17 this summer. Should I tell my mother or I should just keep it a secret?? 17 year old girl.

Dear 'From a different tradition' – You can be very close to someone but you don't need to tell them everything. But you should at least try to explain to your mother about your feelings for this boy before taking any further steps in your relationship with him. She may be more understanding than you think.

Dear Doctor Ann – **I have had epilepsy for the last four years and my Dad doesn't want me to go out with my friends drinking in case I have another attack whilst I'm there.** Boy aged 16.

Dear 'Dad doesn't want me to go out drinking' – **Your dad is trying to protect you in the best way he knows how. You are both going to see this issue from different angles. To reach a compromise you are going to have to promise your dad that you are going to be responsible about your epilepsy and not drink too much when you are out. Reassure him that you understand the limits that your epilepsy puts on you, but that you also want to live the life of a normal 16-year-old. Maybe you could agree to tell your friends all about your epilepsy so they know what to do if you have an attack when you're with them. If you approach this sensibly your dad may let you get on with living your life the way that you want to, but he can only trust you if you avoid doing anything which you know makes the epilepsy worse.**

Dear Doc – **My mum is treating me like I'm a baby and I hate her. Its because I have got asthma.** She doesn't want me to go anywhere smoky in case it brings on asthma attacks. How can I stop her babying me and persuade her that I know what I'm doing? Girl aged 15.

Dear 'Being treated like a baby because you've got asthma' – **You are going to have to be a bit tolerant of your**

mum. I know that you probably realize that she is trying to do what she believes is best for you. The main thing is to talk to her about how you will handle the situations she is afraid of, for example by taking your inhalers etc. If she really understands that you know how to handle yourself – even around people who smoke – then she will be more reassured and let you get on with your life – I hope! And of course you could try to persuade your friends not to smoke, at least near you.

QUARELLING WITH PARENTS

Dear Dr Ann – **my mum and I have been falling out with each other for a few months now and I have been getting really depressed and I have even run away once.** I also feel that if I didn't exist no one would be bothered. Please help me because we fall out over the most stupid stuff like what I want for tea. 14 year old girl.

Dear 'Falling out with your mum' – When you are depressed it can make you feel so bad about yourself that you think no one cares. I'm sure your mum really does care, but the two of you are obviously getting cross with each other over things that shouldn't be causing trouble. Perhaps your mum is worried about other things, which are making her more irritable. Running away isn't going to sort anything out, though I am sure you only did it to try and impress upon your mum you want someone to notice you. Talk to your mum about getting help for your depression.

Dear doctor **can you please help me? I can't stand my mum.** Whenever we are in the same room we end up getting at each others throats. Can i do any thing that will help my mum to listen to me? She isn't like a normal mother! She hardly listens to me!!!!!! Please help me! 14 year old girl.

Dear 'Can't stand my mum' – Most people go through a time when one or other of their parents really irritates them. It is also often true that other people's parents seem much better than your own, but if you did actually swap and  live with these so called normal parents they might turn out to be the same or even worse than your own. Try to talk to your mum and see if you can sort out some of these things that are winding you both up. You need to listen to some of the things she says in return for her listening to you.

Dear Doctor Ann – **My mum and dad split up when I was little.** My mum's married again and had a new baby. My stepdad gets

cross with me all the time cos I don't help with the baby. And I feel really left out. Girl aged 15.

Dear 'Feeling really left out' – I'm really sorry that your parents have split up.

It must make it even more difficult since your mum has had a new baby and doesn't have so much time for you anymore. If you don't want to feel left out, why not talk to your mum about you and her having more time alone together. Then maybe you will feel differently about helping with the baby.

Losing family
members

15

Parents and other members of your family may not
always be there for you. Sometimes parents split up
and very occasionally family members die. This can
cause young people much distress and sadness.

● **WHEN FAMILIES SPLIT UP**

Dr Ann – **my mum and dad split up when I was a baby. Will I ever
see him again.** 14 year old girl.

> *Dear 'Will I ever see my dad again?'* – I am so sorry to
> hear that you don't have contact with your father. You need to
> talk to your mother about your father and explain to her how
> you feel. As young people grow up it becomes
> more and more important to them to know
> exactly who their parents are and what they
> are like – because it helps those young
> people with their own feelings about who they are
> themselves. Explain this to your mother and ask her
> if she has any idea how he might be found. Also
> explain to her that you don't expect her to have any

contact with him – it is just you that needs this. It is quite common for fathers, after a divorce, to lose contact with their children, but I am sure that he would welcome you making the effort to try and contact him– so do have a go.

Dear Ann – **our mum is divorced and she goes out all the time and we never get to see her as she never stays at home anymore.** We miss her a lot and feel that now her affairs out in the open she feels that she can do what she likes and doesn't seem to care about us anymore. On top of all that because our mum is not here our dad makes most of the rules and hardly lets us go out. He only lets us out at the weekend (not including Fridays) and not many of our friends go out on Sundays so the only day we do actually go out is Saturday. Please can you give me some advice. From a frustrated 15 year boy.

Dear 'Mum is divorced' – This must be very difficult for you. My guess is that once your mum has tasted her new 'freedom' she will settle down a bit and start thinking about your needs rather than just hers, so be patient. Your dad may be behaving in a very strict way because he is very unhappy and needs your company more since your mum left. It may also be because he doesn't know or have any experience of how much most 15-year-old boys go out. You need to find a good time to talk to him and try to negotiate a better deal about what you can and cannot do. You might suggest that he talks to some of your friends' parents to get a broader picture of what is reasonable!

Dear Ann – **my parents are divorced and I live with my dad and my grandad and I sometimes feel a bit lonely not having contact with my mom.** I have lots of mates and me and my dad are like best mates. What can I do about feeling empty? 16 year old girl.

Dear 'Feeling empty' – I think that you need, if possible, to make contact with your mum and try to link up with her again. Children and young people want to be able to relate to both their parents, and rather than forgetting about your mum, you might want to try and find her. Don't keep this a secret from your dad – just explain to him how you feel and even ask him if he is able to help you find her. He may still be angry with her if she was the one that left, and he may even feel that you are betraying him by feeling this way, but I'm sure he will understand that you need to do this.

● **SECRETS IN FAMILIES**

Hi doctor Ann. **I am having parent problems. My mum and dad have been married for nearly 15 years but now I have found out that my mum was having an affair.** She made me and my sister swear not to tell our dad and we were stuck in the middle as our dad was asking questions and we didn't know what to do. Eventually they talked between them and now they are separated. But they never talked to us about it. 14 year old girl.

Dear 'Person with a parent problem' – I think it was unfair of your mother to involve you in her affair by asking you and your sister to keep it secret from your father. It's a fact of life that some married people have affairs, but they shouldn't involve their children in any way. Even though your parents have separated, they still need to talk to you about it and explain their reasons. When people split up usually something has gone wrong in the relationship on both sides. When parents split up many children think that they may have been in some way to blame, although of course they were not, and parents need to explain this. Children of separated or divorced parents often feel that if their parents no longer love one another then they will no longer love their children. This is NOT true, but your parents need to reassure you about this and help you understand what's happened between them.

● WHEN FAMILY MEMBERS DIE

Dear Ann – **I recently lost my Gran, Grandad and my big sister in a car crash and feel I can't cope any more.** I find it so hard to talk to my mum as she is hurting too but I have nobody to talk to. Some days I wish I was dead too. I do love life but it just isn't the same without them. Is there someone I can talk to or a group who will know how I am feeling. Please help me. 17 year old girl.

Dear 'Girl who lost Gran, Grandad and older sister in a car crash' – I am so, so sorry about your loss. Do keep trying to talk to your mother and explain your feelings because that may allow her to talk to you about her own feelings as well. I would also suggest contacting your family doctor and asking whether they have a counsellor attached to their practice who you could talk to and who would listen to how you feel. You could also try writing down your feelings because that often helps to put your emotions at a slight distance 'outside yourself' and will help you to work through them.

Dear Dr Ann **I'm a 15 year old girl who can't cope with the state of her family anymore! My dad died when I was 12. My mum is a strict devout Muslim who hardly lets me have a social life and I can't see boys.** She is very strict and I can't take it anymore. I have no real friends that I can confide in coz all they are interested in are problems to do with what they are gonna wear to the next under 18's disco and boys. What should I do? I have been having awful headaches but I don't feel comfortable visiting my GP and every time I try 2 confront my family I lose my nerve or it is not the right time. Please help. I am 15 and depressed.

Dear 'Can't cope with the state of my family any more' – It can be difficult to live in a society where your family has different values and ideas to those in the culture you live in. Unfortunately you're going to have to cope with both of these cultures the best you can. I can understand that confronting your family is very difficult, particularly as you and your mum must still be upset about the death of your father. Your mother might be particularly strict because she's bringing you up on her own. There are many girls in your position so perhaps you could find someone like yourself to talk to about it. The school nurse or your teacher could also be someone to confide in. One way of getting more of a social life without upsetting your mum might be to take part in more school activities. As you get older you will have to confront your mother and family and make decisions that they will not necessarily approve of. But if you think it is right you will have to cope with their disapproval at the same time as letting them know that you still respect their way of life so that they should respect yours.

Need to find out more?

Teenage Health Freak

The Diary of a Teenage Health Freak (3rd edition, OUP 2002)
The book that got it all going. Read the latest version of Pete Payne's celebrated diary in all its gory detail, to find out pretty much all you need to know about your health, your body and how it works (or doesn't – whatever).

The Diary of the Other Health Freak (3rd edition, OUP 2002)
The book that kept it all going. Pete's sister Susie sets out to outshine her big brother with a diary of her own, bringing the feminine touch to a huge range of teenage issues – sex, drugs, relationships, the lot.

Teenage Health Freak websites

www.teenagehealthfreak.org and *www.doctorann.org*
Two linked websites for young people. Catch up on the daily diary of Pete Payne, age 15 – still plagued by zits, a dodgy sex life, a pestilent sister... Jump to Doctor Ann's virtual surgery for all you want to know about fatness and farting, sex and stress, drinking and drugs, pimples and periods, hormones and headaches, and a million other things.

Other websites for teenagers

BBC kids' health
www.bbc.co.uk/health/kids

Mind Body Soul
www.mindbodysoul.gov.uk

Lifebytes
www.lifebytes.gov.uk

NSF young people's project site
www.at-ease.nsf.org.uk

There4me
www.there4me.com

All these sites give lots of information about health, sex and relationships.

All your problems

ChildLine
Royal Mail Building, Studd Street, London NW1 0QW
Freepost 1111, London N1 0BR
Tel: 020 7239 1000
Helpline: 0800 1111 (24 hours a day, every day of the year)
www.childline.org.uk
Provides a national telephone helpline for children and young people in danger or distress, who want to talk to a trained counsellor. All calls are free and confidential.

Alcohol
Drinkline
Helpline: 0800 917 8282 (9 am–11 pm, Mon–Fri; 6 pm–11 pm, Sat–Sun)
National Alcohol Helpline – provides telephone advice, leaflets and information about local groups.

Bereavement
RD4U
Free helpline: 0808 808 1677 (9.30 am–5.00 pm, Mon–Fri)
www.RD4U.org.uk
RD4U is part of CRUSE Bereavement Care's Youth involvement project. It exists to support people after the death of someone close.

Bullying
Anti-Bullying Campaign
185 Tower Bridge Road,
London SE1 2UF
Tel: 020 7378 1446
Gives telephone advice for young people who are being bullied. There are also some websites where you can get help...

Bullying Online
www.bullying.co.uk

Pupilline
www.pupilline.com

Down, depressed, anxious or suicidal
The Samaritans
Helpline: 08457 909090
www.samaritans.org.uk

Someone will always listen to you and your problems any time of the day or night, and it costs nothing for the call.

Eating disorders
Eating Disorders Association (EDA)
First Floor, Wensume House,
103 Prince of Wales Road,
Norwich
NR1 1DW
Youth helpline: 01603 765050 (4–6 pm Mon–Fri)
www.edauk.com
Youth helpline for those aged 18 years and younger. Aims to help and support all those affected by anorexia and bulimia, especially sufferers, the families of sufferers and other carers.

If you are ill
NHS Direct
Tel: 0845 4647
www.nhsdirect.nhs.uk
Talk to a nurse on the phone about any health problem you are worried about.

HIV/Aids
National Aids Helpline
Tel: 0800 567123 (free and confidential; available 24 hours a day, 7 days a week)
Questions or worries about Aids can be discussed with a trained adviser.

Sex and everything attached

www.Ruthinking.co.uk
A great website about sex, relationships and all that stuff.

Brook Advisory Service

Young people's helpline:
0800 0185 023
www.brook.org.uk
User-friendly information service, offering advice on sex and contraception for all young people. Will tell you all about local clinics and send you leaflets even if you are under 16.

fpa (formerly The Family Planning Association)

2–12 Pentonville Road, London N1 9FP Tel: 020 7837 5432
Helpline: 0845 310 1334
(9 am–7 pm, Mon–Fri)
Gives information on all aspects of contraception and sexual health. Free fun leaflets available. They also run a telephone helpline for anyone who wants information on contraception and sexual health. Phone the helpline number to find the nearest fpa clinic in your area.

BAAF (British Agencies for Adoption and Fostering)

Tel: 020 7593 2000
(9 am–5 pm, Mon–Fri)
www.baaf.org.uk
A central agency for organizations involved in adoption and fostering. Publishes useful information leaflets and books about various aspects of adoption. Offers advice on tracing.

Rape Crisis Helplines

Look in the telephone directory or ring Directory Enquiries on 192 for the Helpline number in your area. Provides free confidential support and advice to victims of rape.

Lesbian and Gay Switchboard

Tel: 020 7837 7324 (24 hours a day)
www.llgs.org.uk
(this is the London and national Switchboard; there are also a number of regional Switchboards) Offers information and advice to lesbians and gay men and their families and friends.

Smoking

QUIT

Quitline: 0800 002200 (1 pm–9 pm)
www.quit.org.uk
Want to give up smoking? Phone this line for help.

Index